MAYER SMITH

The Phoenix Queen's Cursed Love

First edition

This book was professionally typeset on Reedsy.
Find out more at reedsy.com

Contents

One

The Arrival of the Curse

The wind howled through the spires of Emberheim, carrying with it a scent that was neither sweet nor foul—something in between, like the last breath of a dying fire. The city sat perched at the edge of the world, a kingdom of ash and flame, where the skies were always tinged with the colors of an eternal sunset. It was a land where the Phoenix Queen, Selene, ruled with a heart both fierce and wary, a queen whose fire had tempered her spirit and hardened her resolve.

But tonight, something was different.

Selene stood on the balcony of her towering castle, gazing out over the city she had sworn to protect. The last remnants of daylight bled into the horizon, staining the clouds in hues of crimson and amber. Her cloak fluttered around her legs, a dark shadow against the flickering light. She had been at the edge of the kingdom for hours, waiting for the signs. Her fingers tingled with an unsettling energy, the same sensation she had felt since the moment the prophecy had arrived—an omen wrapped in black feathers, delivered by an unnamed messenger.

The words of the prophecy echoed in her mind like a haunting melody:

_"A love that will bring both salvation and destruction,
   A heart that will ignite the kingdom's fall,
   A bond forged in fire, a curse that will bind them forever."_

Selene's brow furrowed, her golden eyes narrowing against the wind. The messenger had disappeared as quickly as he had come, leaving nothing behind but a chill that settled deep within her bones. The curse was upon them, and there was no escaping it.

"Your Majesty."

The voice behind her was like the soft flutter of wings, a whisper of caution in the darkness. Selene turned, her expression softening as her trusted advisor, Aroden, stepped into the dim light. His silver hair caught the fading glow of the sunset, his sharp eyes gleaming with intelligence and something darker, something she couldn't quite place.

"What is it, Aroden?" Selene asked, her voice tinged with a quiet tension. She did not need to look at him to know he had been following her for the past few hours. He was always watching, always protective, but tonight, something about him felt different. He was tense, his usual calm demeanor fraying at the edges.

"The council has gathered," Aroden replied, his gaze flickering to the distant horizon, where the sky had begun to darken. "They are asking for your presence. There is talk of unrest among the people, and… rumors of strange happenings in the farthest regions of the kingdom."

Selene nodded, though her mind was elsewhere. "Rumors?" she echoed, her voice distant. "Aroden, what do you think? Is the prophecy true?"

Aroden hesitated, then stepped closer, his voice lowering to a near whisper. "I've been in this kingdom long enough to know that omens are never just omens, Your Majesty. The curse you fear—it is real. And I fear that the one you are meant to love… the one who will either save or destroy us… may already be here."

Selene's heart skipped a beat. The air around her seemed to thicken, pressing down on her chest. She turned away from Aroden, her eyes scanning the city once more, though she saw nothing but shadows and flickers of firelight.

"Who?" she asked, though she had a sinking feeling she already knew the answer. "Who is this person?"

Aroden stepped back, uncertainty clouding his usually unwavering expression. "I do not know, but something stirs in the depths of Emberheim, Your Majesty. It is as if the very earth itself is trembling, waiting for something—or someone—to ignite the fire."

Selene's mind raced. The curse. The prophecy. The words that had been given to her in a vision only weeks before had become all too real. She had tried to dismiss them, to push them from her mind. But now, it seemed that fate had caught up to her.

"I will go to the council," she said finally, her voice firm. "We will face this together. And I will not allow fear to rule me."

But as she turned to leave, a sudden explosion of light filled the sky, blinding her for a moment. A flare of orange and red erupted from the horizon, and the ground beneath her feet trembled violently. The sound of cracking stone and splintering wood reached her ears, followed by a series of distant screams. The city was under attack.

"Your Majesty, we must move quickly," Aroden urged, his hand gripping her arm tightly. "This is no ordinary attack. The curse has begun."

Before Selene could respond, a figure emerged from the shadows, stepping into the flickering light of the balcony. Aroden's grip on her arm tightened as he turned to face the stranger, his expression darkening.

The figure was a man—tall, with dark hair that hung loosely around his face, and a cloak of deep green that billowed around him like a second skin. His eyes, dark and intense, locked onto

Selene's, and for a moment, the world around them seemed to fall away. The air grew thick with an undeniable tension, and Selene felt a pull, deep within her chest, as if the man had just crossed a boundary she had not known existed.

"I've come for you, Queen Selene," the stranger said, his voice low and gravelly, yet oddly familiar. "The curse has already begun, and it is tied to you—and to me."

Selene's heart stopped. The words reverberated through her body, as if they had been carved into her very soul. The prophecy. This was the moment. The man before her—the one who would either save or destroy Emberheim—had arrived.

But who was he?

Aroden stepped forward, his voice sharp with authority. "Who are you? What do you want with the queen?"

The man's eyes never left Selene's, and a faint, knowing smile tugged at the corners of his lips. "I am Raelen," he said simply. "And I am the one who holds the key to your kingdom's fate."

Selene took a step back, her mind spinning. Raelen. The name felt like a distant echo, a whisper she had heard in dreams. The curse. The prophecy. Everything was converging in this moment, and she could not deny it any longer.

"Raelen," she repeated, her voice hoarse. "The curse… It is you?"

Raelen nodded slowly. "Yes, Queen Selene. But you must

understand—this curse is not just mine to bear. It is ours. And together, we must face it."

The wind picked up again, swirling around them like a vortex, as if the very forces of nature were reacting to his words. Selene felt the weight of destiny pressing down on her shoulders. The curse had come. And with it, the man who could destroy everything she held dear.

"Come with me," Raelen said, extending his hand toward her. "It is time to face the truth."

Selene hesitated, a storm of conflicting emotions rising within her. She could feel the heat of the flames in her chest, the fire that had burned within her since birth, but now it felt different— darker, more dangerous. And it was all tied to Raelen.

Aroden's grip tightened on her arm. "Do not trust him, Your Majesty. This is the enemy. The one who will destroy us all."

But Selene's heart was already racing, her pulse quickening as she stepped toward Raelen. The prophecy had spoken of love and destruction. And now, standing before her, was the one who held the power to fulfill both.

With one last glance at Aroden, Selene reached out and took Raelen's hand.

The curse had arrived. And there was no turning back.

Two

Whispers in the Fire

The air was thick with smoke and the stench of burning wood. The once tranquil streets of Emberheim now swirled with chaos. The deep crimson of the setting sun had turned to an ominous shade of red, casting long, eerie shadows across the stone buildings. Selene's heart pounded in her chest, each beat a drum of urgency as she followed Raelen through the crumbling streets. Behind them, the castle loomed like a dark silhouette, its towers now visible through the haze of fire that had begun to consume the kingdom.

"They are coming," Raelen muttered, his voice low and strained, his eyes scanning the smoke-filled horizon. "The fires are only the beginning."

Selene's breath caught in her throat as she glanced at him. He had not yet explained how he knew the curse would unfold, or why he seemed so certain that it would begin with the city's destruction. There was something unnerving in his calmness, an unsettling stillness in the face of the chaos around them.

"What do you mean, 'coming'?" Selene asked, her voice sharp with both fear and command. "Who are they?"

Raelen's gaze flickered to her, his eyes shadowed with a weight that she could not quite understand. He said nothing, but the tension in his silence spoke volumes.

"Raelen, we need answers," Selene pressed, her hand tightening around the hilt of the sword at her side. "I cannot face this alone."

His lips twisted in a tight smile, but there was no warmth in it. "You never were alone, Queen Selene. Not in the way you think."

He stopped abruptly, and Selene almost collided with him. They were standing at the edge of a courtyard now, where the fires had yet to reach, the only light coming from the flickering flames of nearby buildings. A large stone statue of a Phoenix, the symbol of Emberheim's eternal rebirth, stood solemnly in the center of the courtyard, its wings stretched as though it were trying to take flight.

"What is this place?" Selene asked, feeling an unsettling chill creeping up her spine. The place felt ancient, forgotten, and she could sense that something powerful lay buried beneath the stones.

Raelen's voice was barely a whisper. "The Heart of Emberheim. The birthplace of the curse."

Selene frowned. "What do you mean, the birthplace of the curse?"

Raelen stepped toward the statue, his fingers grazing the cold stone. "This city was built on the ashes of the old kingdom, a kingdom whose destruction was set in motion by a similar curse. A curse that burned everything to the ground. That fire—" he paused, his voice growing distant, "—was just the beginning. And this," he motioned to the statue, "was where it began. Where everything is tied together."

Selene's stomach churned as she approached the statue. The air felt heavy here, charged with an unnatural energy that made her skin prickle. She could almost hear the faint whispers of forgotten voices, carried on the wind. What was it about this place? She could feel the weight of centuries pressing down on her, as though the very stones had absorbed the memories of those who had stood here before.

"Why did you bring me here?" she asked, her voice trembling with both frustration and dread.

Raelen met her gaze. "You need to understand the curse, Selene. You need to understand what you're up against."

Before she could respond, a loud crash echoed through the courtyard, followed by the unmistakable sound of footsteps— heavy, deliberate, and many. Selene's heart leapt into her throat, her hand instinctively reaching for the sword at her side. Raelen's eyes narrowed, and he pulled her behind the statue, shielding her from view.

"Stay here," he whispered urgently. "Do not move. Not yet."

Selene's pulse raced, her breath shallow as she crouched behind the cold stone. The sounds of approaching footsteps grew louder, closer. She peered around the edge of the statue, her eyes scanning the shadows for any sign of movement. There was no telling how many were out there, but the air felt thick with the presence of danger.

Then, she saw them.

Figures cloaked in black moved silently across the courtyard, their hoods pulled low over their faces. They were not soldiers, not common men. There was something unnatural about the way they moved, as though they were shadows themselves, gliding between the flames and smoke. The closest figure raised a hand, and Selene could hear the faint whisper of an incantation. The ground beneath their feet seemed to tremble, the earth shuddering with a low, ominous hum.

Raelen's grip tightened on her arm, pulling her back further behind the statue. He glanced over his shoulder, his face pale. "They've come."

"Who are they?" Selene whispered, her voice barely audible.

Raelen's lips tightened into a grim line. "The Harbingers."

"Harbingers of what?" Selene demanded, her mind racing. "What do they want with me?"

Raelen's expression darkened. "The curse is not just a threat to the kingdom—it is a chain that binds you to a fate far older than your bloodline. These Harbingers… they are the keepers of that fate. And they have come to ensure that it unfolds."

A sharp, piercing cry echoed from the distance, cutting through the tension like a blade. Selene's heart skipped a beat. It was a sound she had heard only once before—during her nightmares. A screech so chilling that it froze the very blood in her veins.

The Harbingers stopped in their tracks, their heads snapping toward the source of the sound. The air seemed to thicken with the anticipation of something dreadful.

"Selene," Raelen whispered, his voice tight with urgency. "We need to leave now."

But Selene could not tear her gaze away from the cloaked figures. The Harbingers were still, as though waiting for something, something that only they could hear. A cold sweat dripped down the back of her neck as she realized that she was not merely a witness to this ancient prophecy—she was its focal point.

The leader of the Harbingers, tall and imposing even in the flickering light, lifted his hand, and a wave of dark energy spread outwards. The ground cracked, stone splintering and crumbling as if something were rising from beneath. Selene's breath caught in her throat as she saw the faint outline of a shadow beneath the earth, moving with an unnatural speed. The very earth seemed to groan in response, as though it were alive and responding to the Harbingers' command.

Raelen's grip on her arm tightened, pulling her to her feet. "Selene, we must go, now!"

But the words barely left his mouth before the ground beneath them gave way. A dark, swirling portal opened up before them, its edges crackling with dark energy. Selene stumbled back, her heart hammering in her chest.

"Raelen, what is that?" she gasped.

He was already pulling her away, his face a mask of grim determination. "That is where they want you to go. They are trying to pull you into the past, to trap you in a cycle that has already been set in motion. We can't let them."

But before they could flee, the Harbingers turned as one, their eyes glowing with an eerie light. The leader's voice cut through the air, low and commanding.

"Selene of Emberheim," he intoned, his voice laced with power. "The time has come. The curse cannot be avoided. You will embrace your fate—or perish with the kingdom."

Raelen's eyes flared with panic, but there was nothing he could do to stop the inevitable. The curse had found its way to them. And there was no escaping it now.

The portal's dark tendrils stretched outward, threatening to consume everything in its path.

13

Three

The Wanderer's Heart

The earth trembled beneath Selene's feet as she and Raelen stumbled away from the swirling dark portal. The ground cracked with a sickening sound, as though it were splitting open to reveal the horrors lurking beneath. The Harbingers had not yet moved, their eyes glowing with an unnatural intensity, their presence more imposing than any army Selene had ever faced. The shadows around them seemed to deepen, thickening like ink spreading in water.

Raelen's grip on her wrist was unyielding, his muscles taut as he urged her forward, farther from the growing rift. His breaths came in shallow gasps, and Selene could feel the tension radiating off him like heat from a forge.

"We need to get to the Firekeeper," Raelen said, his voice strained. "Now. There's no time to waste."

The urgency in his tone sent a chill through Selene, one that cut deeper than the fear gnawing at her heart. She had heard whispers of the Firekeeper's power, the ancient sorcerer who had watched over the kingdom for centuries. But even as her thoughts raced, she couldn't ignore the question that kept clawing at her mind.

"What is the Firekeeper to you, Raelen?" she asked, her voice hoarse. "What do you know that you're not telling me?"

Raelen didn't answer immediately, his gaze flickering over his shoulder. The Harbingers were still standing there, motionless, but their presence lingered in the air like a storm waiting to break. His jaw tightened, and Selene could see the muscles in his neck flex as if he were holding back something—something darker.

"I'll explain when we're safe," Raelen said, his voice curt. "But right now, you need to trust me. We don't have the luxury of time."

They ran in silence, the only sound the pounding of their footsteps and the distant crackling of flames that had begun to spread through the city. The streets had grown eerily quiet, save for the occasional distant scream or the ominous thud of something heavy hitting the ground. The people of Emberheim were not fools; they had begun to scatter, fleeing from the chaos that seemed to have erupted overnight.

The castle loomed in the distance, its dark silhouette a beacon in the midst of the chaos. Raelen veered left, pulling Selene down a narrow alleyway, the walls closing in around them. The air smelled of smoke and earth, and the oppressive weight of the curse seemed to press down harder with each step. She could feel it now, like a slow burn in her chest, as though the prophecy was waking inside her, stirring the fire that had been dormant for so long.

"Where are we going?" Selene asked, breathless, as she struggled to keep up with Raelen's long strides. She could see the tension in his back, the way his hands flexed with barely concealed anxiety.

"To the Firekeeper's sanctuary," Raelen replied. "It's hidden beneath the old temple. Only those who are truly bound to the curse can access it."

Selene's eyes widened. "And you're one of them?" she asked, her heart skipping a beat. She had sensed there was more to him than he had let on, but this—this was beyond anything she had imagined.

Raelen didn't respond, but his lips tightened into a grim line. Instead of answering her question, he led her to the entrance of a crumbling temple at the far end of the alley. The stone pillars were shattered, and the roof was partially caved in, but the ancient doors stood intact, an imposing reminder of the temple's former glory. Raelen didn't hesitate; he stepped forward and pushed the doors open with a force that seemed to ripple through the air.

The darkness inside was suffocating, as if the temple itself were holding its breath. Selene stepped inside reluctantly, her pulse quickening as the weight of the place settled over her. The air was thick with the scent of old incense and something far darker—something that lingered like a shadow, just out of reach.

Raelen moved ahead of her, his movements fluid and purposeful. He didn't look back, but Selene could feel his tension growing, his unease radiating from him. She reached out to steady herself against the crumbling stone walls, her fingers brushing against the cool surface. As she did, a faint whisper seemed to echo in the darkness, a voice carried on the wind, just out of her comprehension. It felt like the very walls were alive, whispering forgotten truths to her.

"Raelen," she called softly, her voice breaking the silence. "What is this place? What am I supposed to find here?"

He stopped, his back rigid, as if the question had struck a nerve. Slowly, he turned to face her. The flickering light from the entrance cast shadows across his face, making his features appear sharper, more menacing.

"The Firekeeper is the key," he said, his voice tight. "Without his help, the curse will consume you. It will consume all of us. The only way to stop it is to uncover the truth of your bloodline—of the Phoenix Queen's bloodline."

Selene's heart raced. She knew the legends of the Phoenix Queen—her ancestor, the one who had once saved Emberheim from the brink of destruction. But what did Raelen mean? What bloodline? She felt the stirrings of something deep within her, a strange pull, like a fire smoldering just beneath the surface of her skin.

"What do you mean?" she asked again, her voice barely above a whisper.

Raelen hesitated before speaking again, his voice strained, as if every word was dragging him deeper into something he couldn't escape.

"You were born with the curse already inside you, Selene," he said softly, his eyes locking with hers. "It was always there, waiting for the right moment. The curse is tied to your heart—and to mine."

The air seemed to freeze. Selene's breath caught in her throat. She wanted to deny it, to reject the notion that the curse was truly hers to bear, but the truth in Raelen's eyes—the rawness of it—was undeniable. The curse had been tied to her bloodline, to the very core of who she was, even before she had been born.

"I didn't ask for this," Selene said, her voice trembling with a mix of anger and disbelief. "I never asked for this curse, Raelen. I never asked for any of it."

Raelen stepped closer, his hand reaching out, as if to comfort her, but he stopped short, as if even touching her might ignite something dangerous.

"I know," he said quietly. "But it's too late. We're bound by fate, Selene. And the curse… it's only just beginning."

Before Selene could respond, a low growl sounded from the depths of the temple, a rumble so deep it seemed to come from the earth itself. The air grew colder, the shadows around them lengthening as if something were waking, something ancient and powerful.

Raelen's eyes widened, his expression hardening with a mix of fear and determination. "We have to find the Firekeeper now," he said, his voice urgent. "Before the Harbingers find us."

Selene's heart pounded in her chest as she followed him deeper into the temple, the walls seeming to close in around them. She had no idea what lay ahead, only that the answers she sought— and the curse that haunted her—were somewhere in the dark, waiting to reveal themselves.

Four

A Flame in the Dark

The flickering light from the torch cast strange, elongated shadows on the walls of the ancient temple as Selene followed Raelen through the narrow corridors. The air was thick with dust and the scent of something old, something forgotten. Each step seemed to reverberate through the stone, the sound echoing back at them like a warning. Selene's heart pounded in her chest, the weight of the curse pressing down on her with every breath she took.

She could feel it now, deep in her bones—the unrelenting pull of destiny. The prophecy. The curse. Everything she had fought to deny was coming to fruition, and she wasn't sure whether to run from it or embrace it.

The darkness around her seemed to grow heavier as they descended deeper into the temple's bowels. Raelen led the way, his face set in grim determination, but there was something flickering in his eyes—something that didn't quite match the calm exterior he wore.

They had been walking in silence for what felt like hours, the oppressive silence stretching between them. Selene wanted to ask him so many questions, wanted to demand the answers she so desperately needed. But every time she opened her mouth, she found herself hesitating.

Raelen stopped abruptly, his body tense, his eyes scanning the shadows ahead. A faint noise reached Selene's ears—like the soft scraping of metal against stone.

"Stay close," Raelen whispered, his voice low and urgent. "Whatever happens, do not separate from me."

Selene nodded, her breath catching in her throat. The walls around them seemed to shift, the darkness growing even thicker as if the very temple was alive, watching them. Her fingers tightened around the hilt of her sword, the only thing that seemed to offer any comfort in this place of shadows.

Raelen began walking again, his steps cautious but determined. The passage ahead narrowed, the stone walls closing in as they moved deeper into the heart of the temple. Selene could hear her own breath in the silence, feel the weight of the air pressing down on her. She had always been strong, always relied on her instincts as queen and warrior, but here—beneath the ground, in the heart of this forsaken temple—her instincts were screaming at her to turn back, to flee.

But she couldn't. Not when the truth was so close. Not when Raelen, the man tied to the curse, was by her side.

They reached a large chamber at the end of the passage. The walls were lined with ancient carvings, depicting scenes of fire and ash, of rebirth and destruction. The imagery was familiar—too familiar. The flames that licked the edges of the carvings seemed to move, twisting and curling in the dim light. Selene felt the heat of the fire, not from the carvings, but from deep within her chest.

"This is it," Raelen said, his voice barely a whisper. He stepped into the center of the chamber, where a large stone pedestal stood, covered in dust. On the pedestal lay an object wrapped in tattered cloth—a bundle, small and unassuming. But Selene could feel the power radiating from it.

She took a step forward, her heartbeat quickening. "What is it?" she asked, her voice shaking despite her best efforts to remain calm.

Raelen's eyes never left the bundle. "The key to breaking the curse," he said quietly. "Or the key to your destruction."

Selene felt a cold knot form in her stomach. "What do you mean?"

Raelen's jaw tightened. "The Firekeeper has hidden the truth from you for too long. This is what he's been protecting. The reason why he's kept you in the dark."

Selene's eyes narrowed. "Why didn't you tell me before?"

Raelen's gaze flickered toward her, and for a moment, something vulnerable flashed across his features—something raw, something that made her heart ache. But then it was gone, replaced by the same hardened expression she had seen earlier.

"I didn't trust myself," he said, his voice strained. "And I didn't trust you."

The words hit Selene like a punch to the gut. She opened her mouth to respond, to demand an explanation, but the air around them suddenly grew colder. The shadows in the room seemed to deepen, shifting like a living thing. A low, guttural growl echoed from the far corners of the chamber, sending a wave of cold terror through her.

Raelen's hand shot out to grab her arm, pulling her toward him. "No time for questions now," he growled. "We're not alone."

The growl grew louder, and Selene's heart hammered in her chest. The shadows seemed to stretch toward them, and suddenly, they were no longer alone. Figures emerged from the darkness—tall, cloaked in black, with eyes that gleamed with an unnatural light. The Harbingers.

Selene's blood ran cold. They had found them.

Raelen's grip on her arm tightened, pulling her behind him. "Stay back," he warned, his voice low and commanding. "They're after the key."

The leader of the Harbingers stepped forward, his eyes locked onto Selene's with an intensity that made her skin crawl. His voice was smooth, like silk, but there was no warmth in it. "The curse has already begun, Queen Selene," he said softly. "And you cannot escape it. Not now. Not ever."

Selene's breath caught in her throat. "I will fight you," she said, her voice steadier than she felt. "I will not let you take what's mine."

The Harbinger smiled, a cruel, cold smile that made Selene's blood boil. "You don't understand," he said, his voice carrying the weight of centuries. "What's yours was never meant to be. It was never meant to be yours, Queen Selene."

Raelen moved quickly, pulling Selene further behind him. "Stay out of sight," he whispered urgently. "They want you to face the truth, but you're not ready. Not yet."

Selene barely had time to register his words before the Harbingers began to move, their forms blurring into shadows as they spread out, surrounding them. The leader raised his hand, and the temperature in the room plummeted. A flash of ice-cold energy crackled through the air, and the flames of the torch nearest them sputtered out, plunging the room into darkness.

Raelen's voice was barely audible, but Selene could hear the desperation in it. "Do not engage them, Selene. Not unless you want to die."

But it was too late.

The leader's eyes glowed brighter, like twin orbs of molten gold. "Your death will be a slow one," he intoned. "But first, we will show you the truth."

In an instant, the room was filled with blinding light. Selene staggered back, her hand reaching for Raelen, but the light seemed to push them apart, separating them. The Harbingers moved in, their shadows swirling around her as if they were closing in for the kill.

Raelen's voice called out to her through the haze, his words a faint echo in the chaos. "Selene! You have to fight it! You have to—"

But the words were lost as the world around her began to spin, the shadows thickening, pulling her deeper into a place she couldn't escape. The darkness whispered, and the heat in her chest flared.

The flames of truth were burning, and they would not be quenched until everything was revealed.

And she was standing at the center of it.

Five

The First Sign

The darkness held Selene in its grasp like a vice, cold and suffocating. The swirling shadows that had surrounded her moments before now seemed to crawl under her skin, biting at her senses. Her body trembled, but not from fear. It was the curse awakening, stirring inside her as if it had been waiting for this moment all along. She could feel its power, coiling like a serpent in the depths of her soul.

The blinding light had vanished, leaving only an eerie silence in its wake. For a moment, Selene could only hear the distant pounding of her heart, the rush of blood in her ears, and the sharp breath escaping her lips. She tried to move, to call out to Raelen, but her body felt heavy, as though invisible chains were pulling her down.

"Raelen?" she whispered, her voice hoarse, unsure if she was even speaking aloud.

There was no answer, only the oppressive weight of the shadows pressing in closer, tightening around her chest, squeezing the breath from her lungs. The silence stretched on, suffocating, until it was shattered by the soft crackle of fire.

Her eyes snapped open, and she gasped. The Harbingers were still there, circling her, their eyes gleaming with a hunger she couldn't quite comprehend. Their cloaks moved as if they were alive, twisting and shifting in the air, their edges flickering like flames in the night. The leader, his golden eyes blazing, stepped forward, his movements deliberate and slow.

"Do you feel it now, Queen Selene?" His voice was like ice on her skin, cold and smooth, but full of venom. "The first sign of what you are meant to become. The flames are stirring inside you. You cannot escape your fate."

Selene's breath caught in her throat. The words hit her like a physical blow. The flames—the curse—it was true. It was awakening, just as Raelen had warned. She could feel the heat rising inside her, a fire she could neither control nor deny. It was there, under her skin, racing through her veins like molten lava.

The leader's smile widened, his eyes never leaving hers. "You will learn to wield it, or it will consume you," he said, his voice dripping with cold amusement. "It is already too late to turn back."

She wanted to deny him, to fight, but the truth of his words was undeniable. The heat within her chest flared again, sharp and intense, and she clenched her fists, struggling to keep it contained. She could feel the curse gnawing at her from the inside, clawing its way to the surface.

"You are not ready," she whispered, her voice trembling. "I don't want this. I never asked for this."

The leader's gaze softened, just for a moment, and he tilted his head as if considering her words. "None of us ever ask for the darkness that comes with our power," he said softly. "But you are the Phoenix Queen, and you are bound to the fire. It is your birthright to wield it."

The words settled over her like a weight she couldn't shake. Phoenix Queen. Her ancestor, the one whose blood ran through her veins, had been a symbol of rebirth, a symbol of hope. But that legacy was tied to the curse—tied to this insidious fire that threatened to consume everything. Was this truly her destiny? Was she doomed to live a life of destruction, her every breath fueling the flames that could burn down her kingdom?

Raelen's voice cut through her thoughts, low and urgent. "Selene! You have to fight it. Don't let them control you."

Her head snapped toward him. He was still there, standing just beyond the Harbingers, his face tight with concern. His voice reached her, but it felt like a distant echo, distorted and far away. She could see the flicker of flames dancing in his eyes, and for a moment, she wasn't sure if he was real or a figment of her imagination.

"Raelen!" she gasped, her heart lurching in her chest. She reached out to him, but the Harbingers were closing in, their dark forms surrounding her once more.

"You cannot hide from your fate, Queen," the leader said, his voice like a whisper in her ear. "This is only the beginning. The first sign of what's to come. The fire inside you will grow until it consumes you entirely. There is no escaping it."

A sharp pain shot through her chest, as though the fire within her had ignited in an instant, searing through her skin and straight to her heart. Selene gasped, her breath coming in ragged gasps, her knees buckling beneath her. Her vision blurred, and the shadows around her seemed to stretch, growing darker with each passing second.

Raelen's voice pierced the fog in her mind, urgent, raw. "Selene, listen to me. You are not alone in this. You do not have to succumb to the fire. We can stop it. But you have to trust me."

Trust him. She had trusted him once, hadn't she? She had believed in him, in the bond that had formed between them. But now—now she wasn't sure if she could trust anyone, especially not herself. The fire, the curse, everything felt like it was spiraling out of control, and she was helpless to stop it.

But Raelen's words, his plea, reached her in that moment, and something deep within her stirred. The fire inside her was hers to control, not the Harbingers', not anyone else's. She was the

Queen. She had the power to wield it, to make it her own.

"No," she whispered, her voice gaining strength. "I will not let this curse define me."

The leader of the Harbingers stepped back, his eyes narrowing with a dangerous glint. "You will see, Queen Selene. You cannot fight what is already inside you."

As he spoke, the flames in the room flickered, as if responding to his words, but Selene didn't look away. She felt the fire inside her rise, a surge of heat that burned through her chest, down her arms, into her fingertips. She could feel it, the raw power, the heat, the strength.

"I am the Queen of Emberheim," she said, her voice steady, unwavering. "And I will not bow to the fire. I will bend it to my will."

A blinding light erupted from her chest, so bright that it sent the Harbingers reeling backward. Selene gasped as the flame exploded outward, its warmth enveloping her, not in pain, but in power. The curse was still there, deep inside her, but now it was hers to command. The fire in her veins no longer felt like a threat; it felt like a part of her.

The Harbingers recoiled, their faces twisted with anger and disbelief. The leader's expression darkened, his golden eyes flashing with fury. "No," he snarled. "You cannot control it. It is too late for you."

But Selene was no longer listening. She closed her eyes, focusing on the fire within her, willing it to bend to her will. The warmth spread through her body, filling her with strength and clarity. The curse might have awakened, but she was not its slave.

A sharp gust of wind swept through the chamber, extinguishing the flames that had surrounded them. When Selene opened her eyes again, she saw the Harbingers retreating, their forms dissolving into the shadows as if they had never been there at all.

Raelen was at her side in an instant, his hand on her shoulder. "You did it," he breathed, his voice filled with awe. "You controlled it."

Selene swallowed hard, her body trembling with the aftershocks of the fire that had burned through her. She wasn't sure how she had done it, how she had summoned that power, but she knew one thing: the curse was not her enemy. Not anymore.

But as the last of the shadows faded from the chamber, she couldn't shake the feeling that the first sign of what was to come had only just begun. The fire had been awakened. And now, it was only a matter of time before everything else was consumed by it.

Six

Under the Red Moon

The night sky above Emberheim was an ominous shade of blood-red, casting the land in a strange, unsettling light. The moon hung low, its surface marred by dark veins that pulsed like the heartbeat of some ancient, malevolent creature. Selene stood on the edge of the balcony, staring up at the unnatural glow, feeling a chill in the air that had nothing to do with the temperature. The weight of the curse was heavier tonight, the fire inside her restless, crackling beneath her skin.

She had barely slept since the confrontation with the Harbingers, her mind still racing with the implications of what had happened. The fire—her fire—was a part of her now, something she could control, something that would either save her or destroy her. And yet, every time she thought she had a handle on it, the flames would surge within her, threatening to consume her completely.

Her hand instinctively went to her chest, where the fire seemed to pulse, steady but strong. It was not the same fire that had once been a symbol of rebirth, of hope. No. This fire was darker, more dangerous, and it whispered to her in ways that left her breathless with fear.

A sharp knock at the door pulled her from her thoughts, the sound too quiet to be reassuring. She turned, her heart pounding as her gaze flickered to the wooden door that led into her chambers. The servants had all been sent home for the night, and Aroden had not returned since their earlier meeting. Whoever was knocking had not been expected.

"Come in," Selene called, her voice betraying none of the unease she felt.

The door creaked open, and Raelen stepped into the room. His presence, though familiar, did nothing to ease the tension that seemed to hang in the air. His gaze flicked to the balcony, then back to her. His expression was serious, the concern in his eyes clear despite the stoic mask he wore.

"You shouldn't be out here," he said quietly, his voice low but urgent. "Not with the moon like this."

Selene stiffened, her fingers tightening around the stone railing. "What do you mean?"

Raelen stepped closer, his eyes never leaving the red moon above. "The red moon is a sign," he said. "A sign that the curse is reaching its peak. The first sign was your awakening, but the second… it's coming."

Selene's pulse quickened, and for a moment, she felt the familiar surge of panic in her chest. "What second sign?" she demanded. "What are you not telling me, Raelen?"

He hesitated for a moment before stepping closer, lowering his voice. "The red moon isn't just a celestial event," he said. "It's a marker for the curse's progression. It's a warning that something ancient is stirring, something tied to the very heart of Emberheim. The fire inside you—it's not the only force at work here. There's something darker, something older that is waking with it."

Selene's throat tightened as she processed his words. The fire was one thing—a danger, yes, but one she had started to understand. But this… something older, something darker— she could feel it, deep in her bones, an insidious presence that seemed to tug at the very fabric of her soul.

"What do we do?" she asked, her voice barely above a whisper.

Raelen's eyes met hers, and for the first time since they had met, there was a flicker of uncertainty in his gaze. "I don't know," he said quietly. "But I know this: you're not the only one who has been marked. The curse is not just yours. It's tied to Emberheim itself, to the very land that was built on fire and ashes."

A cold shiver ran down Selene's spine, and she took a step back from the balcony, as though the red moon itself were pressing in on her. "What does that mean? What do you mean by 'marked'?"

Raelen's face darkened, and he clenched his fists at his sides. "I mean that the curse is not just a punishment—it's a call. It calls to those who are tied to it, those who are bound by blood and fire. And it's calling to you, Selene. To both of us."

Before she could respond, a faint sound reached her ears—the soft thud of footsteps from the hall. The door to her chambers burst open, and Aroden stepped inside, his face pale, his eyes wide with fear. He didn't look at either of them immediately, his gaze focused on the red moon outside, his expression grim.

"It's started," he said, his voice barely a whisper. "The land is stirring. The curse is awake, and the first of the Harbingers has already made his move."

Selene's stomach twisted at his words. "What do you mean? Who has moved?"

Aroden finally turned to face them, his eyes dark with an emotion she couldn't place. "The Harbingers are not just agents of the curse. They are its emissaries, its heralds. And now, the first one—the leader of them all—has begun his ritual."

Raelen stepped forward, his eyes narrowing with suspicion. "What ritual?"

Aroden's gaze flickered toward the window, his lips curling into something between a grimace and a sneer. "The ritual that will bind you to the curse forever," he said. "The ritual that will finish what was started all those years ago."

Selene's breath caught in her throat. "What do you mean, 'bind me'? What are you talking about, Aroden?"

Aroden turned to her, his eyes filled with an intensity she had never seen before. "You're the key, Selene. You always have been. The curse… it needs you. Your blood, your fire, your soul. If the leader of the Harbingers succeeds in his ritual, he will bind you to the curse in a way that no one can undo."

Raelen's voice cut through the tension like a blade. "How do we stop it?"

Aroden's eyes flickered between them, and for the briefest moment, Selene saw something like hesitation in his gaze. But it was gone before she could fully register it.

"You can't stop it," Aroden said bluntly. "Not unless you have the key."

Raelen stepped back, his jaw tightening. "What key?"

Aroden glanced back at the window, as if he could feel the very land shifting beneath them. "The heart of Emberheim. The source of the curse. The place where it all began. If you reach it in time, you can sever the curse, destroy it before it destroys you. But it won't be easy. And even if you reach it, you may find that there's nothing left of you to save."

The words hung in the air like a death sentence. The tension in the room was unbearable, thick with the weight of what was to come. Selene could feel it—feel the pressure building, the urgency of the situation. The red moon hung in the sky like a harbinger of doom, and every instinct in her body screamed that time was running out.

"Where is this place?" she asked, her voice steadier than she felt.

Aroden looked at her, his gaze unwavering. "The heart of Emberheim lies beneath the Temple of Ash. But reaching it will not be as simple as walking down a corridor. You will have to confront the curse head-on. And the Harbingers will stop at nothing to ensure you fail."

Raelen's hand found Selene's, his grip firm, grounding her in the moment. "We'll face it together," he said quietly. "Whatever it takes."

Selene's heart hammered in her chest, the flames within her stirring in response to his words. She had never felt so alive, so connected to the power within her. But with that connection came the overwhelming fear that she might not be strong enough to face what was to come. The Harbingers, the curse—everything was closing in.

And the red moon, high in the sky, was the first sign that the end was drawing near.

Seven

The Betrayal

The wind howled outside the castle, rattling the ancient windows as if it too sensed the impending storm. Inside, Selene stood at the edge of the grand hall, her fingers trailing over the cold stone walls as her mind raced. She had known the prophecy since she was a child, heard whispers of it in the corridors, and yet now, standing on the precipice of its unfolding, she felt the weight of it like never before.

The heart of Emberheim, the source of the curse, lay beneath the Temple of Ash. She had to reach it—had to sever the curse before it claimed her, before it consumed the kingdom she swore to protect. But she had no idea how to get there, or what horrors awaited her along the way.

Raelen had gone ahead to prepare, to gather what little information he could about the ritual the Harbingers were performing.

Aroden, too, had slipped away hours ago under the guise of attending to the kingdom's affairs. But Selene knew better than to trust anyone fully now. The air was thick with deceit, and she had begun to wonder just how much of the truth had been hidden from her all along.

The doors to the hall opened, and a shadow stepped into the room, cloaked in darkness. Selene turned, her heart skipping a beat. She had not expected company, certainly not at this hour.

Aroden stood there, his figure barely illuminated by the flickering torches along the walls. His usual composure was gone, replaced by something else—something darker in his eyes. Selene's stomach churned as she watched him step further into the room, his gaze fixed on her with a strange intensity.

"You're late," she said, her voice low but steady. She could feel her pulse quicken, a sense of unease creeping over her.

Aroden didn't respond immediately. He walked toward her with deliberate steps, his expression unreadable. When he finally spoke, his voice was cold, devoid of the warmth and loyalty she had always relied on.

"The Harbingers are already making their move," Aroden said, his voice rough with something she couldn't quite place. "You're running out of time."

Selene raised an eyebrow, crossing her arms over her chest. "Then why do you look like you've just seen a ghost?" she asked, her tone sharp. "What's going on, Aroden? What aren't you telling me?"

For a moment, Aroden's eyes flickered, betraying a hint of something—a glimmer of guilt? But just as quickly, it was gone, replaced by that same icy mask he had worn for years. "I'm doing what I can to protect you, Selene," he said, his words clipped. "But I can only do so much."

Selene stepped closer, narrowing her eyes. "What does that mean? What do you know?"

Aroden hesitated, his gaze flickering toward the door as if expecting someone else to enter. He took a deep breath, then met her gaze, his eyes cold and distant. "You think the Harbingers are the real threat here," he said softly. "You think they're the ones trying to control the curse. But the truth is, it's already too late. The curse is already in you, Selene. It's been there all along."

The words hit her like a blow to the chest, and for a moment, she couldn't breathe. "What are you talking about?" she gasped, taking a step back, her hand instinctively going to the fire that burned in her chest. It seemed to flare at his words, pulsing with an intensity she hadn't felt before.

Aroden's lips twisted into something that could have been a smile, but it was empty, devoid of warmth. "You're the key, Selene," he said softly. "You always have been. The prophecy—it's not about breaking the curse. It's about fulfilling it. And you're the one who will bring it to its true power."

Selene felt her blood run cold, the fire in her chest seeming to burn hotter with each passing second. "No," she whispered, shaking her head in disbelief. "No, that's not true. You're lying. You have to be."

But Aroden's gaze never wavered. "You've always been the Phoenix Queen, Selene. But the curse—it's not a curse. It's a gift. One that has been passed down through your bloodline for generations. And you are the one who will bring the fire to its true form. You are the one who will cleanse the world with it."

The words hung in the air like a death sentence, and Selene's chest tightened with the weight of them. She could feel the fire burning within her, could feel the power that surged through her veins. But was that power truly hers to command? Or was it something darker, something she had been born to unleash?

Aroden's eyes darkened, his voice dropping to a low, menacing whisper. "The Harbingers aren't your enemies, Selene. They're here to help you. They're here to make sure you fulfill your destiny. But the ritual—it must be done. And you cannot run from it."

Selene shook her head, her thoughts spinning. "You're wrong," she said, her voice rising in anger. "I won't let this curse define me. I won't let it control me. I will stop it. I'll find a way."

But Aroden stepped closer, his presence suffocating. "You can't stop what's already inside you. You've been marked, Selene. You've always been marked. And now, you have to make a choice. The fire is yours to wield, or it will consume you."

The words were a challenge, a dare. And Selene felt the fire in her chest respond, rising higher, hotter, until she could no longer contain it. She reached for it, grasping it with all the strength she had, trying to push it back, to control it. But it was slipping through her fingers like smoke, too powerful to be held.

Aroden watched her struggle, his face a mask of calm. "You'll see," he said quietly. "The choice is yours. But the truth is, there is no escape. You were born for this. The prophecy was never meant to be broken. It was meant to be fulfilled."

Selene's vision blurred with the heat of the fire that burned within her, and she staggered back, her breath coming in ragged gasps. The curse had always been a part of her, she knew that now. But was it truly hers to wield, or was it already too late to stop?

As she struggled to control the fire, a voice from the shadows broke through the tension.

"You've made your choice, Aroden."

Selene whipped around to find Raelen standing in the doorway, his eyes locked onto Aroden with a mixture of disbelief and anger. He stepped forward, his jaw clenched tight, the tension between them palpable.

Aroden didn't move, didn't flinch. "You're too late, Raelen," he said, his voice still smooth, but with a hint of something darker. "The curse has already taken hold. There's no way to undo what's been done."

Raelen's eyes narrowed, his expression fierce. "You betrayed her, Aroden," he said, his voice like a growl. "You've been lying to her from the start. You've been playing both sides."

Aroden's lips curled into a thin smile, his eyes glinting with something dark and triumphant. "I've always been playing the right side, Raelen. The side of power. The side of destiny."

"Destiny?" Raelen spat. "This isn't destiny. It's a betrayal."

For a moment, the tension between them was palpable, the air thick with unsaid words and unspoken threats. Selene stood frozen, torn between the two men who had both played such a crucial role in her life.

Finally, Aroden's gaze flicked back to Selene, and the mask of indifference returned. "The fire is yours, Selene," he said, his voice softening. "You just have to accept it. And you'll see, everything will fall into place."

With that, Aroden turned and walked out of the room, leaving Selene and Raelen standing in the tense silence that followed.

Selene's breath came in shallow gasps, her chest tight with the weight of the choice before her. She had always believed that she could control the fire within her, that she could break the curse. But now, with Aroden's words echoing in her mind, she wasn't sure if she could ever escape what had been set in motion.

Raelen stepped forward, his hand gently resting on her shoulder, grounding her. "We'll face this together," he said quietly. "Whatever it takes."

But in her heart, Selene knew that the path ahead was darker than she could ever have imagined. And the fire that burned inside her was not the only thing she had to fear.

Eight

The Flamekeeper's Secret

The walls of Emberheim's ancient halls echoed with the sound of hurried footsteps as Selene paced back and forth in the quiet of her chamber. Outside, the dark sky pressed down like a heavy blanket, the red moon casting its eerie glow over the land. The fire within her chest had not cooled since Aroden's betrayal; if anything, it had grown hotter, more insistent. Her skin burned, and her mind was a battleground, the flame fighting to take control of her thoughts, her very soul.

Raelen had left hours ago, in search of answers. He had said the Firekeeper held the key to unlocking the curse, but Selene wasn't sure she could trust anyone anymore. The Firekeeper had been an enigma, a figure who had always remained in the shadows, his true role in the kingdom uncertain. But now, with Aroden's treachery weighing heavily on her mind, Selene knew that finding the Firekeeper was no longer a choice—it was a necessity.

The door to her chamber creaked open, and a figure stepped inside, cloaked in shadows. Selene's heart skipped a beat, but she didn't flinch. If there was one person she could still trust, it was Raelen.

But when the figure emerged from the darkness, it wasn't him.

It was Aroden.

Her breath caught in her throat, and for a moment, she couldn't speak. The audacity of him, to walk back into her chambers after everything that had happened… after his betrayal. Anger rose within her like a tidal wave, but she bit it back, forcing herself to remain composed.

"What do you want, Aroden?" Selene demanded, her voice low and sharp. "You've already made your choice. You've chosen the curse. You've chosen your path. So why are you here?"

Aroden didn't answer right away. Instead, he closed the door behind him with a soft click, locking them both in the room. His eyes were cold, calculating, but there was something else in them now—something that sent a shiver down Selene's spine.

"I'm here because you're running out of time, Selene," Aroden said, his voice eerily calm. "The curse is already on the verge of consuming you. The fire within you is growing stronger, and it's only a matter of time before it consumes not only your mind but your very body. But I can help you. I can make sure you don't lose control."

Selene's fists clenched at her sides, her nails digging into her palms. "And why would I trust you?" she asked through gritted teeth. "After everything you've done?"

Aroden took a step closer, his presence overwhelming. "Because you have no other choice. Because, deep down, you know I'm the only one who can save you."

His words hung in the air like a noose, tightening around her chest. Every instinct in her screamed to push him away, to strike him down where he stood. But the fire inside her... it didn't listen to reason anymore. It raged, burning hotter with each passing second, whispering that the only way to control it was to take the power for herself. And Aroden was right about one thing: time was running out.

"What do you want from me?" she asked, her voice trembling, but with a new edge of desperation.

Aroden's lips curled into a thin smile, but it was not a smile of comfort or reassurance. It was the smile of a man who knew something she did not. "The Firekeeper holds the key," he said. "But he's not going to give it to you willingly. You've been searching for answers your whole life, Selene, but now that the truth is within reach, you'll have to make a choice. The question is, are you ready to accept it?"

The room seemed to close in on her as Aroden's words sank in.

The Firekeeper. A figure who had remained elusive, a shadow that haunted the corners of the kingdom, never fully known but always present. Selene had thought she understood the nature of the curse, but now, in the face of Aroden's words, she felt like she was standing at the edge of a precipice, staring into the abyss.

"What is the truth?" she whispered, her voice hoarse. "What am I not seeing?"

Aroden stepped closer, his eyes gleaming with something dark, something ancient. "The Firekeeper is not just a guardian of knowledge, Selene. He's the keeper of a secret that goes back centuries. A secret that's tied to the very origins of Emberheim. And you are at the center of it."

Selene took a step back, her heart pounding. "What do you mean?"

Aroden's smile deepened. "I know where he is. I can take you to him."

Selene felt a flicker of hope, but it was short-lived. The doubt gnawing at the edges of her mind, the suspicion that Aroden was leading her into a trap, lingered like a shadow. She had trusted him once. She had believed in him. But now, the truth seemed just out of reach, hidden behind a veil of lies and manipulation.

"Why should I trust you?" Selene asked again, her voice cold now, every word dripping with suspicion.

Aroden's eyes darkened. "Because you don't have a choice. If you want to survive this, if you want to control the fire inside you, you need to face the Firekeeper. But be warned, Selene. The truth comes with a price."

The words hit her like a dagger to the heart. She had always known that there was a price to pay for power, for the curse that flowed through her veins, but hearing it spoken aloud made the reality of her situation all the more terrifying.

"You've already made your choice, Selene," Aroden continued, his voice low and persuasive. "The path ahead is fraught with danger, and there is no going back. The Firekeeper can show you how to control the flames, but he will not do so without taking something in return."

"I don't need your help," Selene said, her voice rising with defiance. "I will find the Firekeeper on my own."

Aroden's expression darkened, and for a moment, the mask of calm he wore slipped. "You're already too far gone," he said quietly, almost to himself. "The flames are inside you, and they're getting stronger by the second. You're already feeling it, aren't you?"

Selene's chest tightened, and the fire within her flared in response to his words. She could feel it—pulsing beneath her skin, waiting to explode. But now, as Aroden's words echoed in her mind, she knew he was right. She had no more time to waste. The flames were becoming unbearable, and she needed the Firekeeper's secret. She needed to know how to control it before it consumed her completely.

With a final glance at Aroden, Selene made her decision. "Take me to him," she said, her voice steady, her resolve hardening like steel. "But know this, Aroden: if you betray me again, I will destroy you."

Aroden's lips curled into a smile that didn't reach his eyes. "Very well, Queen Selene. Let's see if you're truly ready for what lies ahead."

And with that, he turned, leading her into the darkness, where the truth—and the curse—awaited.

Nine

Through the Ashen Sea

The cold wind bit at Selene's skin as she stood at the edge of the cliff, the vast expanse of the Ashen Sea stretching before her like an endless, turbulent expanse of darkness. The salt air stung her nostrils, mingling with the acrid scent of ash that rose from the jagged, volcanic rocks at the base of the cliff. Above her, the dark sky swirled with crimson clouds, the ominous red moon casting its sinister glow over the landscape. The night felt wrong—unnatural, as though the very earth itself was holding its breath.

Behind her, Aroden stood motionless, his eyes fixed on the horizon. The weight of the journey hung heavily between them, an unspoken tension that neither of them dared to address. Selene could feel the heat of the curse pulsing within her chest, a constant reminder of the path she had chosen. The fire that had once been a symbol of power was now a threat, a monster growing within her, threatening to consume her very essence.

The Firekeeper was close. He had to be. The answers Selene sought—answers about the curse, about her bloodline, about the fire inside her—were locked within the heart of the Ashen Sea. The Firekeeper had hidden there for centuries, waiting for someone worthy to come and seek him out. But Selene wasn't sure if she was ready. The price of the truth was high, and she could feel the cost of it gnawing at her.

"Are you ready?" Aroden's voice broke the silence, his tone flat, distant. He had not said much since they had left Emberheim, and Selene could feel his unease like an undercurrent beneath his calm exterior.

She turned to him, her eyes narrowing. "Why did you bring me here, Aroden?" she asked, her voice low and steady. "What are you really trying to achieve? You've already betrayed me once. Do you think I can't see through your lies?"

Aroden met her gaze, his expression unreadable. For a moment, there was nothing but the wind and the distant sound of crashing waves below them. Then, he spoke, his voice quieter now, as though revealing something he had kept hidden for far too long.

"I didn't bring you here for my own gain, Selene," he said. "I brought you here because it's the only place left where you can find the truth. The Firekeeper's secret is the only thing that can save you. It's the only thing that can save Emberheim."

The words hung in the air, thick with implication. Selene's breath quickened, her pulse pounding in her ears. "And what is the secret, Aroden?" she demanded. "What is it you're not telling me?"

Aroden's eyes flickered for a brief moment, a shadow passing over his face. "It's not my secret to tell," he said, his voice tight. "You'll have to ask him yourself. But I will warn you, Selene. What you learn here—what you uncover—may change everything. It may change you."

Selene could feel the weight of his warning pressing on her chest, but she pushed it aside. She had come this far. There was no turning back now. She needed the answers, needed to understand what had been hidden from her all these years.

With a final glance at Aroden, she turned back to the Ashen Sea, her gaze fixed on the swirling mists that hovered just above the water. The Firekeeper was somewhere out there, hidden in the depths. She could feel his presence, a dark, powerful force that seemed to pulse beneath the surface, waiting for her to find it.

As if responding to her thoughts, the air around them shifted. The wind picked up, howling like a thousand voices whispering in the distance. The water below them began to churn, the surface roiling as though something massive was rising from the depths.

Aroden took a step back, his face pale as he watched the water. "It's starting," he said, his voice low. "The ritual has begun."

Before Selene could react, the ground beneath them trembled. The earth seemed to shift, as if the very foundation of the world was cracking open. The rocks around them cracked and splintered, and with a deafening roar, a massive wave surged from the Ashen Sea, crashing against the cliffside.

Selene's heart leapt into her throat as the wave surged higher, its force shaking the very earth beneath her feet. Aroden grabbed her arm, pulling her back as the water surged around them, swallowing the cliffside with a ferocity she had never seen. For a brief moment, she felt herself being pulled toward the edge, the pull of the water almost too strong to resist.

But then, as quickly as it had come, the wave receded, leaving only the sound of the crashing waves and the eerie silence of the night. The air was thick with tension, and Selene could feel the weight of something heavy hanging in the air.

Aroden's grip tightened on her arm as he pulled her toward the edge of the cliff. "We need to move," he said urgently. "The Firekeeper is close. But he's not the only one."

Selene turned to him, her eyes wide with fear. "What do you mean?" she asked, her voice trembling.

Aroden's gaze shifted to the horizon, his face grim. "The Harbingers," he said, his voice barely above a whisper. "They're coming. They've followed us here."

Selene's stomach dropped, and for the first time since they had left the castle, fear gripped her heart. The Harbingers had been a constant shadow in her life, and now, they were closing in on her once more. But this time, she wasn't the same woman who had run from them before. She was stronger, more powerful. But would it be enough?

Before she could respond, a dark shape appeared on the water, cutting through the mist like a knife. The water parted around it, revealing the figure of a massive ship, black as night, its sails tattered and torn. A low, mournful horn sounded from the ship, and Selene felt a cold shiver run down her spine.

Aroden's grip tightened on her arm as he pulled her back from the cliff's edge. "We need to go," he said, his voice urgent. "Now."

Selene turned to him, her heart racing. "Why? What's happening?"

Aroden didn't answer. Instead, he turned and began to walk away from the cliffside, pulling Selene with him. She followed, her mind spinning, her thoughts a whirlwind of confusion and fear. What was happening? Who was on that ship? And why was Aroden so determined to get her away from it?

They reached a narrow path leading down toward the base of the cliff, and Aroden pushed forward with an urgency that left no room for hesitation. Selene's thoughts raced as she followed him, the sound of the crashing waves growing louder behind them.

They reached the bottom of the cliff, where the path widened into a small clearing, and Aroden stopped suddenly, his eyes scanning the shadows. "We're almost there," he said, his voice tense. "Stay close."

But as they stepped deeper into the clearing, a figure emerged from the darkness. Tall, cloaked in black, with eyes that glowed like molten gold.

Selene's breath caught in her throat as she recognized the figure. It was one of the Harbingers.

Before she could react, the figure stepped forward, raising his hand as a wave of dark energy pulsed through the air. Selene felt the fire inside her flare in response, the heat surging as if in answer to the threat before her.

Aroden's voice cut through the tension. "Do not engage, Selene," he warned, his voice tight. "This is not the time."

But it was already too late. The Harbinger's eyes locked onto hers, and in that moment, Selene knew that the battle for Emberheim, for her very soul, had only just begun.

Ten

The Heart of the Curse

The air around Selene was thick with tension, and the fire within her chest seemed to burn hotter with each passing second. The Harbinger stood before her, his dark cloak swirling like a shadow in the flickering light of the dying torches. His eyes, molten gold, glowed with an eerie intensity, watching her every move. For a moment, everything was still—the night air, the churning sea, even her own breath seemed to freeze in place, waiting for something to break the silence.

Raelen had been silent since the Harbinger's arrival, standing just behind her, his body tense, his hand subtly resting on the hilt of his sword. Selene could feel the weight of his gaze on her, a reminder that she was not alone in this, even as the power inside her continued to grow.

The Harbinger's voice broke the stillness, low and rich with authority. "Selene, Queen of Emberheim, you stand at the precipice. The curse calls to you. You can feel it, can't you? The flames inside you. The blood of the Phoenix runs through your veins."

Selene's breath hitched, her heart hammering in her chest as the heat in her body surged. She could feel it—like a furnace burning from within her. The curse, the fire—it was all tied to her, and in this moment, it felt as though the flames were taking over, urging her to embrace the darkness that called to her soul.

The Harbinger stepped closer, his voice a whisper of silk. "You are more than you know. The power that flows through you is ancient, and it is yours to command. But only if you accept your fate. Only if you let the fire consume you."

Her throat tightened, and for a moment, she thought she might fall to her knees under the weight of it all. Could she really allow herself to be consumed? Could she give in to the fire that had already scarred her from within?

Raelen's voice cut through the oppressive silence, his words filled with a quiet but determined fury. "You won't control her. She won't fall for your lies."

The Harbinger's eyes shifted to Raelen, his gaze cold and calculating. "You think you can protect her? You think you can stop what is coming? The curse is not something that can be bargained with, Raelen. It is not something that can be undone."

Selene's gaze flicked to Raelen, her heart aching at the fear in his eyes. He had always been there, always protected her from the darkness. But this—this was different. This was something beyond them both. The curse was part of her, tied to her bloodline, to the very essence of Emberheim. And the Harbinger was right: there was no escaping it.

But Selene wasn't ready to give up—not yet. She clenched her fists, fighting the flames that clawed at her insides. "I won't let it consume me," she said, her voice strong, despite the tremble in her chest. "I will not give in to this. The fire inside me is mine to control, not yours."

The Harbinger laughed, a sound that was cold and mirthless. "You still don't understand. You can't fight it, Selene. The curse has already marked you. The fire inside you is your inheritance, your destiny."

The wind howled around them, picking up speed as if to echo the Harbinger's words. Selene could feel the ground beneath her tremble as if the earth itself was reacting to his words. The fire inside her surged, threatening to break free of its restraints. It clawed at her, demanding release, demanding she surrender.

Raelen stepped forward, placing himself between Selene and the Harbinger, his sword drawn, the blade shimmering with a cold light. "You will not have her," he growled. "Not today, and not ever."

The Harbinger's expression darkened, his eyes narrowing with disdain. "You think your weapon will stop me?" he sneered. "You think you can fight what is inevitable?"

A low, guttural growl escaped the Harbinger's lips as his body began to ripple with dark energy. The air around him seemed to warp, the shadows deepening in response to his power. With a flick of his hand, a tendril of darkness shot toward Selene, aiming to wrap around her, to seize her with the full force of the curse.

Selene's heart pounded as the tendril reached for her, but in that moment, something inside her snapped. The fire that had been simmering within her suddenly erupted, bursting outwards in a violent surge of power. Her body burned with the intensity of it, the flames inside her leaping out, turning into a fierce blaze that engulfed her in light.

The tendril of darkness recoiled as if burned by the heat of her power, and Selene felt the curse within her surge to life. It was both terrifying and exhilarating, the fire wild and untamed, but it was hers. It was part of her, and for the first time, she felt a sense of control over it.

She raised her hands, and the flames responded to her, swirling around her like a storm of fire and light. The Harbinger stepped back, his eyes wide with a mixture of surprise and fury. "Impossible," he snarled. "You should be bowing to the curse, not wielding it."

Selene's chest heaved with the effort of controlling the fire.

It was a struggle, a constant battle to keep the flames from consuming her completely, but she wasn't going to let it control her anymore. She would fight, not just for herself, but for Emberheim, for the people who depended on her.

The ground beneath them began to crack, the earth splitting open as if reacting to the power of the curse. From the depths of the rift, a low, rumbling sound emanated, like the voice of the land itself, awakening from centuries of slumber.

Raelen turned to Selene, his expression grim. "We need to stop him," he said urgently. "We can't let him summon the full power of the curse. You're the only one who can stop him."

Selene nodded, her gaze never leaving the Harbinger. She could feel his dark energy pulling at her, trying to drag her into the depths of despair, but she refused to succumb. The fire inside her was not just a weapon—it was her strength, her defiance.

With a cry, Selene thrust her hands forward, sending a wave of fire toward the Harbinger. The flames roared as they swept across the ground, lighting the earth in a blinding flash of light. The Harbinger raised his hands, a barrier of shadow forming before him, but the fire slammed into it with an explosive force, breaking through the darkness with a crack that echoed through the air.

The Harbinger staggered back, his cloak billowing around him as if he were caught in the wind. For a moment, the air was thick with smoke and heat, and Selene's vision blurred from the intensity of the flames. But she didn't stop. She couldn't stop.

The fire surged again, this time more controlled, more focused. The Harbinger cried out as the flames burned through his dark barrier, scorching the very air around them. He raised his hands in desperation, summoning dark energy to shield himself, but it was too late. The flames consumed him, surrounding him with the heat of the curse, bending it to Selene's will.

For a moment, there was only the sound of crackling fire and the heavy silence that followed. The Harbinger fell to his knees, his body trembling with the force of the flames. Selene's chest heaved with the effort, the fire still raging inside her, but under her control.

She stepped forward, her eyes locked on the fallen Harbinger. "You were wrong," she said, her voice steady and filled with authority. "The fire does not control me. It is mine to command."

The Harbinger's gaze met hers, his eyes filled with rage and disbelief. "You cannot defeat the curse, Selene," he hissed. "It is eternal. It will consume you, just as it has consumed all who came before you."

Selene raised her hand once more, the fire at her command, but she didn't release it. Not yet. Instead, she let the flames flicker, letting the heat settle around them like a warning.

"You're wrong," she said again, her voice calm but fierce. "I am not the curse. I am its end."

And with that, she let the fire consume the Harbinger, erasing his dark presence from the world.

The flames died down, leaving only the smoldering remnants of the battle behind. Selene stood, her breath shallow, her body trembling with the effort. The fire within her was still alive, but it was hers now. And for the first time, she felt like she had control.

Raelen stepped forward, his hand gently resting on her shoulder. "You did it," he said softly, his voice filled with awe. "You truly did it."

Selene nodded, her eyes scanning the horizon, where the red moon still hung heavy in the sky. But the battle wasn't over yet. The curse still called to her, still whispered in her soul. And she knew that the true test had only just begun.

Eleven

Beneath the Ashen Skies

The night air felt suffocating, thick with the weight of what had just occurred. The fire had faded from her body, but the heat still lingered in her bones, a reminder of the power she had unleashed. Selene stood at the edge of the cliff, looking down at the smoldering remains of the Harbinger, his body reduced to little more than ash, his dark power extinguished. But the victory felt hollow, the silence around them oppressive, as if something worse still awaited.

The red moon hung low in the sky, casting a bloody light over the Ashen Sea, its waves now eerily calm, as if even the ocean had drawn back in fear of what Selene had done. The fire within her still churned, restless, pulling at the edges of her mind, like a beast on the verge of breaking free. She had controlled it—she had forced it into submission—but at what cost?

Aroden's words echoed in her mind: "The truth will change you, Selene. It may destroy you."

The weight of those words pressed down on her, a suffocating burden. She had thought that finding the Firekeeper would bring clarity, but instead, all she had uncovered were more questions. The curse that had once seemed so simple, so straightforward, had revealed its true nature—and now she was no longer sure who she was, or what she was meant to become.

Raelen approached quietly from behind, his presence a comforting one, even as it brought a new tension. His steps were measured, his gaze never leaving the horizon, where the remnants of the Harbinger's dark power still lingered in the air like a fading storm cloud. He stopped a few paces away, his eyes narrowing as he studied her.

"You did what needed to be done," Raelen said softly, his voice low but full of conviction. "The Harbingers are gone. The curse... for now, it's broken."

Selene didn't respond, her gaze fixed on the ashes that were all that remained of the Harbinger. The truth was, she didn't feel any closer to breaking the curse than she had before. The fire inside her had only intensified, its power stronger than ever, and the more she tried to control it, the more it seemed to slip from her grasp.

"What if it isn't over?" she murmured, her voice barely audible.

Raelen stepped forward, his hand brushing against her shoulder, a reassuring touch that brought a small measure of comfort. "It's not over," he said, his tone serious. "But you've shown them that you're stronger. You've shown the curse that you can fight it."

Selene's eyes darted to him, her heart pounding at the intensity of his words. "Stronger?" she echoed bitterly. "Stronger than what? Than the very essence of the curse itself? Than the fire that burns inside me? Raelen, I'm not sure I can control this much longer. The fire… it's growing. Every time I use it, it takes more of me."

Raelen's expression darkened, his hand lingering on her arm, grounding her. "I won't let you face this alone, Selene. You don't have to carry this burden by yourself."

A tremor passed through her, not from fear but from the overwhelming sense of power that surged through her veins. She had never felt so close to the flame, so intertwined with it. And yet, it terrified her. She feared that one day it would consume her, just as it had consumed those who had come before her.

"There's something I need to show you," Raelen said, pulling away from her slightly, his gaze turning toward the rocky outcrop where a narrow path descended into the valley below. "Follow me."

Without another word, he began walking toward the path, his footsteps steady. Selene hesitated only a moment before following. Despite the uncertainty that gnawed at her, she knew that this was the only way forward. If the answers she sought were out there, buried beneath the weight of the curse, then she had no choice but to seek them.

The path was treacherous, winding through jagged rocks and thick underbrush, the shadows of the night growing deeper with each step. The eerie red light from the moon filtered through the trees, casting long, distorted shadows across the ground. The silence was unnerving, broken only by the occasional rustle of leaves or the distant crash of waves against the cliffs. It felt as though the very land was holding its breath, waiting for something.

Raelen led her to the base of the cliffs, where the ground sloped downward into a hidden valley. A crumbling structure loomed ahead—an ancient temple, its walls weathered and cracked, its once-grand arches now reduced to skeletal remains. The air around it was heavy with the same oppressive energy that Selene had felt when she first encountered the Firekeeper. The sense of foreboding was palpable, as though the temple itself was alive, holding onto secrets it had guarded for centuries.

"This is it," Raelen said, his voice barely above a whisper, his eyes scanning the temple. "The Temple of Ash."

Selene's heart skipped a beat. She had heard the legends, of course. The Temple of Ash was where the curse had begun, where it had been forged in the fires of an ancient ritual. But she had never imagined that she would stand here, at the very heart of it all.

"This is where it all began," Raelen continued, his gaze shifting to the ruins before them. "Where the first Queen of Emberheim embraced the curse to save her kingdom. And where the Firekeeper has hidden the answers we need."

As they moved closer, the weight of the temple's presence seemed to grow heavier. The very air around them seemed thick with the remnants of ancient magic, a magic that had once bound Emberheim to the curse—and now, it seemed, it might hold the key to breaking it.

Selene stepped forward, her fingers brushing against the cracked stone as she entered the temple. Inside, the air was musty, thick with dust, but there was a strange warmth to it, as though the walls themselves still held the fire of a long-dead power. The chamber before them was vast, the ceiling lost in shadow, the stone floor uneven and cracked. But at the center of the room stood an altar, its surface still pristine, untouched by time.

Raelen moved toward the altar, his expression grim. "The Firekeeper will be here," he said, his voice low. "But he will not come willingly. He never does."

As if on cue, the temperature in the room dropped. A soft rumble echoed through the chamber, and the flames that flickered in the torches along the walls suddenly flared to life, casting flickering shadows across the stone. The air shimmered, and from the darkness at the far end of the temple, a figure appeared—a tall, hooded figure, his presence commanding and ancient.

Selene's breath caught in her throat as the figure stepped into the light. His face was obscured by the hood, but there was no mistaking the power that radiated from him, an aura of knowledge and darkness that seemed to fill the room.

"You seek answers," the Firekeeper's voice echoed, deep and resonant. "But the truth comes at a cost, Queen Selene. Are you willing to pay the price?"

Selene felt the fire inside her flare, and for the first time since she had met Raelen, she knew what she had to do. The answers lay within the Firekeeper, but she would not let him control her. She was the one who wielded the fire now. She was the one who would decide her fate.

"I will face whatever cost comes," Selene said, her voice steady, her gaze unwavering. "But I will not bow to the curse. I will not be its slave."

The Firekeeper tilted his head, a faint smile curling beneath his hood. "Very well, Queen of Emberheim," he said softly. "Let us see if you are truly ready to face what lies beneath the Ashen Skies."

And with that, the room seemed to shift, the air thickening with the weight of a thousand forgotten secrets. The truth, Selene realized, was no longer a distant goal—it was here, waiting to be uncovered. But whether she was ready for it, she wasn't sure.

The cost of knowledge was more than she had anticipated. And the flame within her was not the only thing she had to control.

Twelve

The Price of Truth

The air inside the Temple of Ash was thick with the scent of ancient incense and the faint, acrid odor of burning embers. The Firekeeper stood before Selene, his dark hood obscuring his face, but she could feel his gaze on her, as if his very presence was pressing against her, searching for weaknesses. She could feel the weight of the room closing in, the stone walls towering above them like silent sentinels. It was a feeling of entrapment, as if the very temple was alive, watching, waiting.

Raelen stood behind her, his presence a silent reassurance. His hand brushed lightly against hers, grounding her in the midst of the gathering storm that raged inside her. The fire within her chest flared, its heat threatening to explode, yet she forced herself to remain calm. For the first time, she felt as though the flames were not just part of her—they were her. She was the fire. And now, she needed answers.

The Firekeeper's voice, when it came, was deep and resonant, carrying a weight that seemed to reverberate in her bones.

"You seek the truth, Queen Selene," he said, his tone calm but laced with an unsettling undercurrent. "But truths have a price. And not all truths are worth the cost."

Selene's pulse quickened. The words, spoken with such certainty, chilled her to the core. She had expected this—expected him to test her resolve—but even so, hearing the warning fall from his lips made her feel vulnerable, exposed. Was she prepared to face whatever lay behind the mask of the curse? Or was she about to make a mistake she would regret?

Raelen stepped forward, his voice firm. "We've come this far, Firekeeper. We need to know what holds Selene's soul. What lies beneath the curse. If there's a way to break it—or at least control it—we need that knowledge."

The Firekeeper's eyes glinted beneath his hood, his mouth curling into a faint smile. "Control?" he murmured. "Control is an illusion, Raelen. The flame, the curse—it is a force of nature. It cannot be controlled. It can only be channeled or consumed."

Selene's heart pounded in her chest. The Firekeeper's words struck too close to the truth. She had already felt the fire gnawing at her, threatening to consume her will, to drown her in its power. Could she really master it? Could she avoid becoming a slave to the curse?

She swallowed hard, her voice steady but edged with a defiance she didn't entirely feel. "I will not let the fire control me. I will choose my path, no matter the cost. Tell me what I need to know."

The Firekeeper was silent for a long moment, his eyes flickering with something that might have been amusement—or perhaps pity. He raised one hand, the motion slow and deliberate, and in the darkness of the temple, the air seemed to crackle with energy.

"Very well," the Firekeeper said at last. "You will have the truth. But be warned: once you see what lies beneath the curse, you cannot unsee it. The truth is a burden, one that cannot be cast aside once it is known."

He stepped aside, and with a gesture, the ancient altar in the center of the room flared to life. A jagged beam of light shot from the altar, casting strange, shifting shadows across the walls. The flames that had once seemed to burn with an uncontainable fury now simmered, their glow darkening as if responding to the Firekeeper's will. The very air around them pulsed with dark energy, the silence suffocating.

"Look into the heart of Emberheim," the Firekeeper intoned, his voice low and commanding. "See the truth of the curse that binds you."

Selene's breath caught in her throat as she stepped forward, compelled by the strange energy radiating from the altar. The fire inside her surged, reacting to the pull of something ancient, something buried deep beneath the earth. She could feel it, like a whisper against her skin—a call, a beckoning.

She reached out, her fingertips brushing the surface of the altar. The moment she made contact, her vision blurred, and the world around her seemed to dissolve. The shadows stretched and twisted, and for a brief moment, she felt herself falling, tumbling into an abyss of light and flame.

Then, everything stilled.

Selene was no longer in the temple. She stood on the edge of a vast, fiery landscape, the ground beneath her cracked and blackened, the sky above burning with the intensity of a thousand suns. The air was thick with heat and ash, and the flames rose around her, reaching out like hungry hands. But amid the fire, something else moved—something alive—an ancient, pulsing energy that she recognized at once.

The heart of Emberheim.

She had heard the stories, of course—the legends of the Phoenix Queen, the one who had sacrificed herself to save the kingdom, the one whose blood had bound the fire to the land. But now, standing on the edge of the inferno, the truth hit her with the force of a hammer.

She was the fire.

Her breath caught in her throat as the landscape around her shifted, revealing the twisted, charred remains of an ancient city. Towering spires of stone, once proud and majestic, now lay crumbling, reduced to rubble by the relentless flames. The ruins stretched out before her, the skeletons of buildings rising from the ash like the forgotten graves of a long-dead civilization. And in the center of it all stood a massive, glowing forge, the heart of the fire that had consumed everything.

"This is where it all began," a voice whispered, faint but unmistakable. It was the Firekeeper's voice, but now it sounded distant, as though it was coming from somewhere far below.

Selene's heart hammered in her chest as she approached the forge. The flames within it flickered and shifted, their light shimmering with an unnatural brilliance. The fire was alive, its heat unbearable, its power palpable. She could feel it, sense it, as though it were reaching into her very soul.

"The curse," the voice continued, "was never meant to be broken. It was born from the deepest fires of Emberheim. It is the lifeblood of the kingdom itself. And you, Queen Selene, are its final vessel. You were born to carry it, to wield it, to become it."

Selene stepped closer to the forge, her body trembling with the weight of the truth. She could feel the fire, surging within her, threatening to overtake her. The flames reached for her, trying to draw her in, to claim her. But she didn't let them.

"I won't be your puppet," she said through gritted teeth. "I won't let the curse control me."

But the voice only laughed, the sound like the crackling of a thousand flames. "You cannot fight what is inside you, Selene. You were born of the fire. It is in your blood. It will consume you, no matter how hard you fight. You are already bound to it."

A surge of heat rushed through Selene, and for a moment, she felt as though the flames were burning her alive. But she fought, pushing against the fire, willing it back, willing it to stay within her, to be hers. And slowly, the flames began to recede.

"No," she whispered, her voice fierce. "I will control it."

The vision flickered, the landscape shuddering, and suddenly, she was back in the temple, her hand still resting on the altar. Her breath came in ragged gasps, and her chest burned with the intensity of what she had just witnessed. The truth—the fire, the curse—was more than she had ever imagined. It wasn't just part of her. It was her.

She looked up at the Firekeeper, her eyes blazing with determination. "You're right," she said, her voice steady despite the storm inside her. "I was born to wield the fire. But I will choose how I wield it. I will not be its slave."

The Firekeeper's eyes gleamed, and for the first time, Selene saw something like respect in his gaze. "Then you have made your choice," he said softly. "But know this: The fire you carry is ancient, and it will test you in ways you cannot yet understand. The price of truth is steep, Queen Selene. You will pay it, and the price will not be light."

Selene nodded, the weight of his words sinking deep into her soul. But she had made her choice. The fire was hers to command, not the other way around. And no matter what the price, she would face it.

The true test was only just beginning.

Thirteen

The Edge of Despair

The temple's stone floor felt cold beneath Selene's feet as she stood, rooted to the spot, staring at the Firekeeper. His words echoed in her mind, his warning about the fire she carried, the power that surged beneath her skin, always threatening to consume her. The price of the truth was steep, and the burden weighed heavily on her. But as much as she feared the consequences of this cursed inheritance, she could no longer deny its existence. The fire was hers to wield—or be destroyed by it.

She clenched her fists, the familiar burn of heat pulsing just beneath her skin. It was as though the flames were testing her resolve, coaxing her to let go, to surrender to their power. The mere thought of losing control was enough to send a cold shiver down her spine.

The Firekeeper watched her, his face shadowed beneath his hood, his expression unreadable. "You think you can master this power," he said, his voice a soft rumble, "but it will only break you in the end. The fire inside you is a reflection of Emberheim itself. It is both the kingdom's salvation and its ruin. To wield it is to walk the line between creation and destruction."

Selene's heart raced, and her gaze darted to Raelen, standing at the edge of the altar, his eyes fixed on her. There was concern in his gaze, but also something else—something she hadn't seen before. Fear.

Raelen stepped forward, breaking the tension that seemed to suffocate the air. "You've given her no choice but to face it," he said, his voice hard, but with an edge of protectiveness. "She's already carrying the curse. Whether she masters it or not, the flames are hers to control."

The Firekeeper's lips twisted into a faint, almost imperceptible smile. "Ah, yes. The protector. But even you, Raelen, cannot change what is inevitable. She was born for this, as was the first queen of Emberheim. And just like her, Selene will be consumed if she does not let go."

Selene's breath caught in her throat. The Firekeeper's words hit close to home. She had always been different, always felt the weight of her bloodline, the legacy of the Phoenix Queen burning in her veins. But was she truly bound to the fire? Or could she break free from the curse that had been woven into her existence?

"I will not be consumed," Selene said, her voice cold and defiant, as she turned her gaze back to the Firekeeper. "I will wield this power on my own terms. I refuse to become a puppet to a fate I never chose."

A flicker of amusement passed through the Firekeeper's eyes. "You have no choice, Selene. Fate does not bend for the weak. You were always meant to be the flame, and when the time comes, you will burn, as all things tied to the curse must."

The room seemed to shift around her, the very air thickening with oppressive heat. Selene felt a sudden, overwhelming urge to escape, to flee from the weight of the Firekeeper's words. But she couldn't run. She had never been a coward, and now was no different. She could feel the fire within her, pulsing like a second heartbeat, pushing her forward. There was no turning back.

"I'm done running," Selene said firmly, her voice steady despite the storm raging within her. "If I must burn, then so be it. But I will not let the flames take everything from me."

As soon as the words left her mouth, the temperature in the room skyrocketed. The flames within her surged, bursting to the surface with a violent, uncontrollable force. She gasped, her hands trembling as the heat swirled around her like a living thing, licking at her skin. The fire was no longer something she could control with mere thought; it was alive, hungry, and demanding.

Raelen's eyes widened in shock as he stepped back, a worried expression crossing his face. "Selene, no! You're losing control!"

Selene's chest rose and fell rapidly as she struggled to breathe through the suffocating heat. The fire was threatening to consume her once more, but this time, something felt different. There was a strange pull to it, a connection she had never experienced before. The flames were her, and she was the flames. But the cost of that connection was starting to unravel her.

"Focus, Selene," Raelen's voice pierced the chaos, steady and insistent. "You have to control it, or it will consume you!"

She squeezed her eyes shut, trying to center herself amid the roaring inferno inside her. The power surged through her, filling her mind with visions of firestorms, of destruction, of everything she had ever known burning to ash. She could feel the Firekeeper's presence watching her, waiting, as if he were testing her, judging her every move.

Raelen's hand reached out, grasping her arm gently but firmly, pulling her back to him. The contact seemed to break the immediate hold of the fire, and for the first time since the flames had consumed her, she was able to draw a full breath.

"Raelen, help me," she whispered, her voice strained, her body still trembling with the aftershock of the fire. She couldn't do this alone. The fire was too powerful, too consuming. It was testing her, and she feared that if she failed, she would never be able to regain control.

Raelen's grip tightened, his voice soft but urgent. "Selene, listen to me. You are in control. The fire is yours, but you must focus. You have to find the center of it, the part of you that is not consumed by it."

She nodded, clenching her fists, drawing all of her focus inward. The flames burned through her mind like a wildfire, but deep inside her, she could feel the steady pulse of something else—a heartbeat that was hers, a steady rhythm that didn't falter in the face of the storm. She clung to that pulse, that constant center of her being, and slowly, the flames began to recede.

The air in the temple shifted, the temperature slowly returning to normal as Selene regained control. Sweat trickled down her brow, but she remained standing, her hands still trembling with the remnants of the fire that had consumed her.

The Firekeeper watched her silently, his face unreadable. Finally, he spoke. "You have passed the first test, Queen Selene. You are stronger than I anticipated."

But Selene didn't feel stronger. She felt hollow, exhausted, as though the very marrow of her bones had been scorched. "What do you want from me?" she demanded, her voice quiet but firm. "What is the price of the truth you promised?"

The Firekeeper took a step closer, his gaze never leaving hers. "The truth comes with a sacrifice, Selene. You will need to make a choice. The fire inside you cannot be controlled without consequence. You will either master it, or it will master you."

Her stomach twisted at his words. "And if I fail?" she asked, dreading the answer.

The Firekeeper's smile was faint but knowing. "If you fail, Selene, everything you love will burn. And you will burn with it."

The weight of his words pressed down on her like a vice. Raelen's presence beside her was the only thing keeping her grounded, but even he couldn't shield her from the truth that the Firekeeper had revealed. The flames were not just part of her—they were the key to everything, to her future, to Emberheim's survival. And if she failed to control them, it wouldn't just be her that burned.

For the first time, Selene truly understood the cost of the curse she carried. The price of truth was not one she was ready to pay—but she had no choice. The flames were her burden, and the kingdom's fate was bound to her success.

As the Firekeeper stepped back into the shadows, leaving her with nothing but the weight of his words, Selene knew that the battle was far from over. The hardest test was yet to come.

And time was running out.

Fourteen

The Breaking of the Flame

The night was unnaturally quiet, the kind of stillness that crept under your skin and made every breath feel too loud. Selene stood at the edge of the temple's precipice, the wind whipping around her, but it was the heat she felt most—the insidious, suffocating heat that had become a constant companion. It radiated from within her, an unrelenting reminder that the fire was not just part of her. It was her.

The Firekeeper's words haunted her, echoing in her mind like a death knell: "You will either master it, or it will master you."

The temple had become a cage, its walls closing in on her with every passing moment. The flames inside her churned, seeking an escape, an outlet, and she was its prison. She had thought she could control it, had believed that by accepting the curse, she could bend it to her will. But now, standing on the edge of everything, she wasn't so sure.

Behind her, Raelen lingered in the shadows of the temple's entrance. His presence was always steady, a quiet anchor in a world that seemed to be spiraling out of control. But tonight, even he couldn't quell the rising tension between them. The fire had become a barrier, not just to her, but to the fragile connection they shared.

"Selene," Raelen called softly, stepping forward, his voice carrying the weight of something unspoken. "It's time."

Her chest tightened, and she glanced back at him. "Time for what?" The words escaped her before she could stop them, the bitterness in her voice betraying the uncertainty she felt deep within.

"You know what I mean," Raelen said, his gaze steady. But even his eyes, usually filled with unshakeable trust, now betrayed a hint of worry. "The path to breaking the curse… it's not going to be easy. The Firekeeper showed you the truth. You've seen it yourself—the flames, the destruction that follows."

Selene nodded but said nothing. The truth had been laid bare before her—unforgiving, relentless, and all-encompassing. She had chosen to embrace it, but that choice came with a cost. Now, the fire inside her burned brighter, threatening to swallow everything she had once believed in. She had seen the vision of the land consumed by flames, of Emberheim reduced to ash, its people scattered like the embers of a dying fire. And she knew that if she couldn't control the flame, she would become the very thing that destroyed it.

Raelen closed the distance between them, his hand reaching out, touching her shoulder with a gentleness that surprised her. "I know you're afraid," he said quietly. "But this isn't just about the curse. It's about who you choose to be."

She jerked away from his touch, the fire inside her flaring at the sudden shift of emotion. "I don't have a choice, Raelen. You don't understand. This power—this curse—it's not something I can just control. I can't just… let it go. I can't be what you want me to be."

Raelen's expression softened, but there was a stubbornness in his eyes. "What I want for you is for you to survive this. To reclaim the person you were before all this madness. Before the curse took hold of you."

A hollow laugh escaped her lips, more from desperation than humor. "Before? You think I can go back to what I was before? Before Emberheim was cursed? Before this fire consumed me?" Her voice cracked, the rawness of her words cutting through the stillness. "I am the curse, Raelen. And there's no escaping that."

Raelen's eyes softened, but he remained silent, as though unsure what to say. The silence between them grew thick, heavy with the weight of their unspoken fears. For a moment, Selene wondered if she had lost him—if the fire had driven him away, the way it had slowly been driving her away from everything she had ever known.

But then, as if drawn by an invisible thread, Raelen stepped forward once more, his presence like a shield against the storm that raged inside her. "You're not the curse," he said, his voice firm. "You're Selene—Queen of Emberheim, the one who was destined to rise from the ashes. You are the fire, yes. But you are also its master, not its servant."

Selene shook her head, her chest tight with emotion. "I don't know if I can do this, Raelen. I don't know if I'm strong enough to control it. The fire—every time I use it, it feels like it's taking more of me. The flames—they control me, not the other way around."

Raelen's gaze never wavered. "You are strong enough," he said. "But you're right about one thing—you can't fight the fire by denying it. You need to accept it, Selene. Not control it. Be the fire."

The words hung in the air, an impossible truth that felt just out of reach. Be the fire. How could she possibly accept something that had nearly consumed her, something that threatened to burn her and everyone around her?

As if answering her unspoken doubts, the ground beneath her feet trembled, a low rumble vibrating through the temple. Selene's heart skipped a beat as the flames inside her roared to life once again, responding to the tremors, as though the very earth were calling out to her. She closed her eyes, fighting the panic rising in her chest, trying to steady her breath.

But it was no use.

The fire surged through her, wild and untamed, and Selene could feel the heat rising inside her until it threatened to overwhelm her. The air crackled with energy, and the temple's walls seemed to pulse with the intensity of the flames that burned within her. The fire was hers, yes, but it was also a part of the land, a force that had been born of Emberheim's very foundation.

She stumbled backward, her hands trembling as she fought to keep control. "Raelen…" Her voice faltered. "It's too much."

Raelen was there in an instant, his hand on her arm, his voice a steady anchor in the chaos. "You've already done the hardest part. Now you have to let go. Let the fire be a part of you, not your enemy."

Her eyes filled with tears as she looked at him, the strength in his gaze both a comfort and a burden. How could she let go of something so powerful, something so dangerous? How could she trust herself with such destructive potential?

"I'm scared," she whispered, her voice barely audible over the roar of the flames. "What if I lose myself?"

Raelen's face softened, his expression filled with compassion. "You won't lose yourself, Selene. The fire doesn't define you. You do. You're the one who decides who you are. And you're not alone. I'll be with you every step of the way."

Selene nodded slowly, her heart aching with the weight of his words. She closed her eyes, taking a deep breath as she let the flames inside her rise once more. She felt the fire pushing against her, testing her, but this time, instead of fighting it, she leaned into it. She opened herself to it, letting it fill her, not as a destructive force, but as a part of who she was.

The flames roared around her, but they no longer felt like enemies. They felt like a storm, wild and untamable, but beautiful in their raw power. She could feel them within her, a part of her very essence. She was not the fire, but she was one with it.

The temple trembled again, this time more violently. The ground cracked beneath their feet, and the walls seemed to cave in on themselves, the stones groaning as though the entire structure was coming to life. Selene opened her eyes to find the temple in chaos, the shadows shifting and warping around them.

"Raelen, what's happening?" she gasped, panic rising in her chest.

"This is it," he said urgently, pulling her toward the altar. "You've done it, Selene. You've unlocked the heart of the curse. But now, we need to act. The fire—Emberheim—it's all connected. You have to destroy the source before it consumes everything."

The ground shook again, the force of the tremor nearly knocking them off their feet. The air was thick with heat and darkness, and the flames surged around them, as though the very land itself was responding to Selene's command.

But now, she was ready.

With a steady breath, she closed her eyes, summoning the flames within her. She was the fire now, not its slave, and she would wield it. The time for hesitation had passed.

The flame would burn, but it would not burn her.

It would burn away the curse.

Fifteen

The Phoenix's Choice

The air was thick with the scent of ash and the crackling of dying embers as Selene stood before the altar, the flames around her flickering with a life of their own. The ancient temple shook violently as if protesting the weight of her decision, the very stones groaning beneath the pressure. Raelen stood beside her, his gaze fixed on her with a mixture of concern and awe, but there was something else there too—something that spoke of uncertainty. He had seen the power she wielded, but even he could not know the full cost of that power.

The Firekeeper, now silent and watchful, stood in the shadows of the temple, his dark presence looming over them. He had warned and told her that the truth would come at a price. But Selene had refused to turn back. She had made her choice. She would be the master of the flame, not its servant. But standing here, with the temple falling apart around her and the fire surging through her veins, she couldn't shake the feeling that the price was more than she could afford.

She closed her eyes, breathing in the heavy, heated air as the flames inside her flared. The power was intoxicating—wild, untamable—but beneath it all was a gnawing sense of fear. What if she couldn't control it? What if the fire consumed her, just as it had consumed all those before her? The thought lingered in her mind, cold and insistent, like a shadow waiting to strike.

Raelen's hand rested on her shoulder, his touch grounding, steady. "Selene," he whispered, his voice filled with a quiet urgency. "You have to act now. The fire's reaching its peak. If you don't destroy the source, the curse will consume everything. Emberheim. Us."

Her breath hitched in her throat as his words sank in. She had come so far, but now the weight of the decision bore down on her like a mountain. Destroy the source, or be destroyed. It wasn't just the kingdom at risk. It was everything she had ever known—her people, her home, her very soul.

She turned to him, her eyes wide, the fire in her chest flickering violently in response to the turmoil within her. "I don't know if I can do this, Raelen," she admitted, her voice barely above a whisper. "I don't know if I can bear the cost."

Raelen's eyes softened, but there was no hesitation in his voice. "You are the fire, Selene. You've always been. The curse isn't just a burden—it's part of who you are. You can do this. I believe in you."

Her heart ached at his words, the love and trust in his eyes pulling her toward him, but the flames inside her raged against the calm, pulling her in a direction she couldn't fully control. She turned away, her gaze once again fixed on the altar, on the heart of the curse that pulsed before her.

It was then that she saw it—felt it. The flames that surrounded her were no longer just hers to command. They had merged with the very essence of the temple, of Emberheim itself. The fire was part of the land, part of her bloodline. The first queen of Emberheim had forged this curse with the sacrifice of her soul, binding it to the very heart of the land. And now, Selene stood at the crossroads, the final heir to that cursed legacy, the last one who could either destroy it or let it consume everything.

The flames pulsed, and she could feel the heart of Emberheim beating with her own. It was as if the land itself was alive, reaching for her, pulling her deeper into the fire. A voice echoed through the chamber, ancient and familiar, but full of a darkness that chilled her to the bone.

"Selene," the voice whispered, low and insistent. "You are the flame. You are the Phoenix, reborn from the ashes. But to destroy the curse, you must first destroy yourself."

The words were like a knife to her heart. The choice was clear— sacrifice herself, let the flames consume her in order to save her kingdom, or become the flame, allowing it to burn everything she loved until there was nothing left. Her breath came in shallow gasps, her fingers curling around the altar's edge as the weight of her decision threatened to suffocate her.

Raelen stepped closer, his voice cutting through the roar of the flames that threatened to engulf her. "Selene, you don't have to make this sacrifice alone. Whatever happens, I'm with you. I always will be."

She turned to him, her eyes filled with unshed tears, but her resolve began to solidify. She couldn't let the fire control her any longer. She had been born of it, yes, but that didn't mean it had to define her. She would be the one to control it, not the other way around. And in doing so, she would find a way to save Emberheim—not just from the curse, but from the darkness that had always threatened to consume it.

"I don't know if I can save everyone," Selene whispered, her voice trembling with the weight of the decision. "But I can't let this curse go on any longer. I won't let it destroy everything. I won't let it take you, Raelen."

Raelen's eyes softened with something that was almost fear, but also a deep, unshakeable faith. "You are the fire, Selene. And the fire is what will save us all."

The Firekeeper's voice echoed once again, this time more insistent, more commanding. "The cost is high, Queen Selene. The flames will not be tamed without sacrifice. You will be consumed by it. The land will burn, and you will burn with it. There is no escaping this fate."

Her heart raced in her chest as she stepped forward, her feet carrying her closer to the altar. The flames pulsed with a strange, rhythmic energy, like a heartbeat, and with each step, she felt the pull of the fire grow stronger. She could feel the essence of Emberheim, feel it calling to her, drawing her deeper into its core.

The fire was not a burden. It was her birthright. It was who she was. And in that moment, Selene made her choice. She would embrace the flames, not to destroy herself, but to transform. She would be the Phoenix, reborn—not just from the ashes, but from the very heart of the curse itself.

With a final breath, she raised her hands, feeling the fire surge within her like an explosion, and as she did, she felt the heart of the land pulse in time with her own. The temple trembled, and the air grew heavy with the weight of what was to come. The ground beneath her cracked, the sky above darkening as the power of the curse rose up to meet her.

The flames spiraled out from her body, tearing through the temple, breaking free from their ancient bonds. They reached for the sky, for the very soul of Emberheim, and for the first time, Selene felt the fire bend to her will. It no longer threatened to consume her—it was hers to command.

But with that power came the cost. She felt her strength draining, her very essence burning away, and in that moment, she understood the Firekeeper's warning. To wield the flame was to walk a razor-thin line between life and death. The sacrifice was not just of her body—it was of her soul.

She cried out as the fire surged around her, but she did not let go. She embraced it, knowing that this was the price she had to pay. The land trembled, the flames rising higher, and for a brief moment, it felt as though the world itself was on the brink of destruction.

But then, everything stopped.

The fire fell silent, and the world seemed to hold its breath.

Selene stood there, her body trembling with exhaustion, her mind reeling from the power she had just unleashed. The temple was still standing, the fire no longer raging, but something had changed. She could feel it—the land was no longer bound to the curse. The flames that had once threatened to consume Emberheim now burned with a purpose: to protect, to transform, to create.

She had done it. She had saved them all.

But as the fire died down, Selene collapsed to her knees, her strength fading. Raelen rushed to her side, his hands gentle as he cradled her in his arms. "You did it, Selene," he whispered, his voice breaking. "You saved us."

But even as she looked up at him, something inside her stirred— a deep, burning pain that she could not ignore.

The price had been paid.

And Selene knew, in that moment, that she would never be the same again.